Collage

Sue Nicholson

QED Publishing

Copyright © QED Publishing 2005

First published in the UK in 2005 by
QED Publishing
A Quarto Group company
226 City Road
London EC1V 2TT

www.qed-publishing.co.uk

A Catalogue record for this book is available from the British Library.

ISBN 1 84538 162 9

Written by Sue Nicholson
Designed by Susi Martin
Editor Paul Manning

Publisher Steve Evans
Creative Director Louise Morley
Editorial Manager Jean Coppendale

The author and publisher would like to thank:
Sam, Georgina, Christopher and Emily
Sarah Morley for making the models
Evie Fitzpatrick for the body collage on page 13

Printed and bound in China

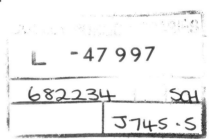
Note to teachers and parents

The projects in this book are aimed at children at Key Stage I and are presented in order of difficulty, from easy to more challenging. Each can be used as a stand-alone activity or as part of another area of study.

While the ideas in the book are offered as inspiration, children should always be encouraged to work from their own imagination and first-hand observations.

All projects in this book require adult supervision.

Sourcing ideas

★ Encourage the children to source ideas from their own experiences as well as from books, magazines, the Internet, galleries or museums.
★ Prompt them to talk about different types of art they have seen at home or on holiday.
★ Use the 'Click for Art!' boxes as a starting point for finding useful material on the Internet.*

★ Suggest that each child keeps a sketchbook of their ideas.

Evaluating work

★ Encourage the children to share their work and talk about their ideas and ways of working. What do they like best/least about it? If they did it again, what would they do differently?
★ Help the children to judge the originality of their work and to appreciate the different qualities in others' work. This will help them to value ways of working that are different from their own
★ Encourage the children by displaying their work.

* Website information is correct at the time of going to press. However, the publishers cannot accept liability for information or links found on third-party websites.

Contents

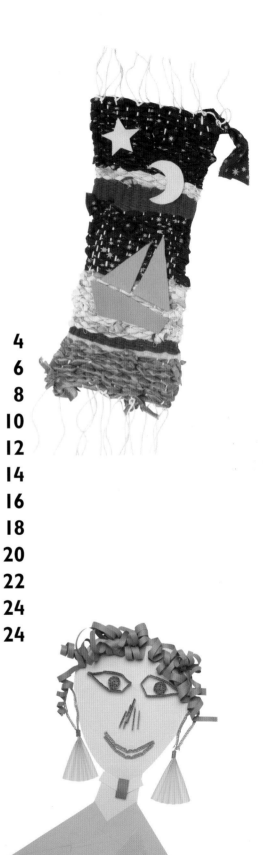

Words in bold, **like this**, are explained in the Glossary on page 24.

Getting started

A collage is a picture made from scraps of paper or other materials. You can use anything in a collage, from cardboard and string to sequins – but be sure to ask first!

Here are some of the things you will need:

Top tip
Don't forget to spread out some newspaper to work on, and wear an apron to keep your clothes clean.

Paper
You can use all sorts of paper in your collages. Collect:

- Newspaper and magazines
- Shiny card
- Tissue and tracing paper
- Crêpe paper, brown paper and **sugar paper**
- Wallpaper and sandpaper
- Lacy doilies, used stamps and sweet wrappers

Safety scissors

Basic equipment

- Paper and card
- Poster/**acrylic** paints
- Pencils and paintbrushes
- Safety scissors
- **PVA glue** and sticky tape
- Ruler

You will also need some extra items which are listed separately for each project.

Collage box

Keep a box to collect objects and materials with an interesting **texture** or shape – like buttons, beads, wool, string or bubble wrap. See the list on page 14 for more ideas.

Glue

Sticky tape

For your backing sheet

- Thick piece of cardboard
- Sides cut from a cardboard box

Get weaving!

You can **weave** your own cloth to use in your collages. Turn to page 20 to find out how it's done.

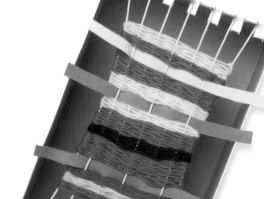

Take care!

Collage projects often involve cutting, gluing and spraying. When cutting, always use safety scissors, and ask an adult to help you where you see this sign:

5

'Me' collage

Tell a story about yourself through a collage. The **theme** could be a birthday, a favourite hobby, a holiday – or how about your favourite things?

You will need:

- Materials for your collage
- Thick cardboard backing sheet

1 Collect together things that tell a story. If you're not sure what to do, look at the red and blue boxes on these pages for ideas.

Top tip

Always ask an adult for help with cutting and gluing.

Football collage ideas

A football collage could include

★ Team photos
★ Scraps from a football programme
★ Ticket stubs from a match
★ Newspaper headlines about football stars
★ Fabric from an old football shirt
★ Football boot laces or studs

3 Stick down all the things to your backing sheet with PVA glue. Glue a small area at a time.

2 Arrange all the things you have collected on a thick cardboard backing sheet. Move them around until you are happy with the way they look.

Click for Art!

To see a photocollage by David Hockney, go to **http://artlex.com/** and search on 'Photocollage'.

Fun collage made from ticket stubs, postcards and other holiday souvenirs

Holiday collage ideas

★ Photographs from travel brochures or magazines
★ Ticket stubs
★ A sprinkling of sand and shells
★ Ice-cream wrappers
★ Postcards and stamps
★ Foreign coins

Magazine collage

Make a collage from scraps cut or torn from magazines. Choose a theme you find interesting – this one is about food. Look at the Collage themes box for other ideas.

Collage themes

★ Animals   ★ Flowers
★ Ballet   ★ Football
★ Cars   ★ Happiness
★ Colours   ★ Horse-riding
★ Dinosaurs   ★ Robots
★ Dogs   ★ Space
★ Faces   ★ Winter

You will need:
- Plenty of old newspapers and magazines
- Thick cardboard for the backing sheet

1 Find pictures in magazines about your theme. Using safety scissors, cut out as many pictures as you can.

2 Arrange the pictures on your backing sheet until you like the way they look.

3 Glue the pictures onto the backing shee

Click for Art! To see a collage by Picasso, go to www.tate.org.uk click on 'Collection', then search on 'Picasso' and 'Bottle of Vieux Marc, Glass, Guitar and Newspaper'.

3D pictures

To make a picture stand out from the backing sheet:

1 Glue the picture onto thick card. Cut out the card around the picture.

2 Fold a strip of card in half, then in half again. Open it out a little, so it looks like a chair with the bottom folded under.

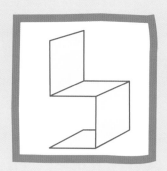

3 Glue the flat part at the top to the backing sheet.

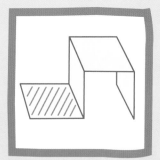

4 Glue the picture to the raised part that sticks out at the front.

Food collage using pictures cut from magazines

9

Paper collage

You can use all sorts of paper in a collage. Collect plain coloured paper, wrapping paper, wallpaper, sweet wrappers, tissue paper, sugar paper and newspaper.

paper parrot

Top tip
Try using transparent coloured paper so the top colour mixes with the colour below.

I Plan your picture first. Draw the picture lightly in pencil on the white card backing sheet.

This parrot has been made from different kinds of paper, cut into shapes then glued in place.

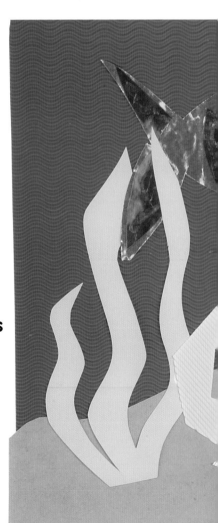

Click for Art!
To see a collage by Matisse, go to **www.tate.org.uk** click on 'Collection' then search on 'Matisse/The Snail'.

10

2 Using safety scissors, cut out the different kinds of paper into the shapes you want for each part of the picture.

3 Move the pieces of paper around on your drawing until they look right.

4 Glue down the paper shapes, one at a time. To overlap shapes, glue larger pieces first, then smaller ones on top.

Fish shapes cut from foil

Tissue paper strips for seaweed

Sandy seabed cut from fine sandpaper

Collage face

The collage face on page 13 is made from cardboard that has been cut, folded and rolled in different ways.

The collage face on page 13

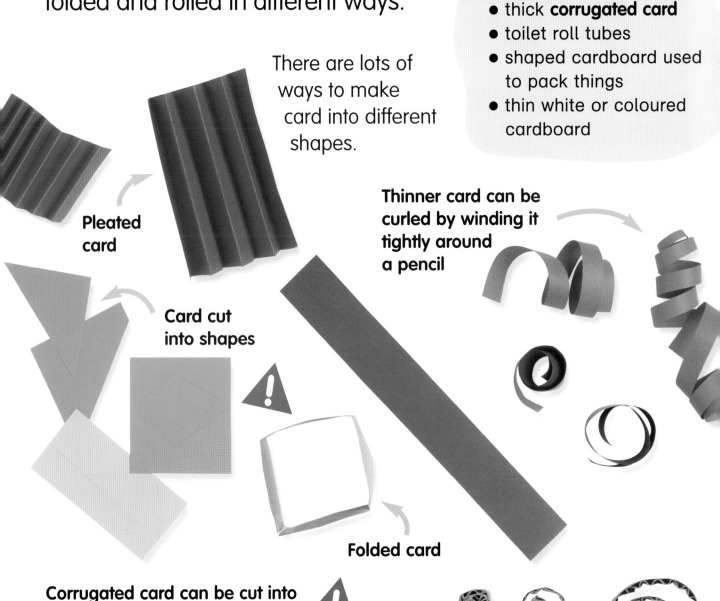

There are lots of ways to make card into different shapes.

Cardboard crazy!

How many types of cardboard can you find?
Try collecting:

- empty food boxes
- eggboxes
- thick **corrugated card**
- toilet roll tubes
- shaped cardboard used to pack things
- thin white or coloured cardboard

Pleated card

Card cut into shapes

Thinner card can be curled by winding it tightly around a pencil

Folded card

Corrugated card can be cut into a shape and stuck down flat ...

... or cut into a long strip and rolled into a tight circle ...

... or a loose spiral that sticks up from the backing sheet

Life-size body collage

Hair made of thin, green card, rolled into spirals

Ask a friend to lie down on a long piece of paper and draw around him or her with a pencil. Lightly draw in the face. Glue down lots of different materials such as wool, fabric, felt, torn paper, sequins or ribbons to make the face and clothes.

Eyes made out of tightly rolled corrugated card

Card glued in wavy lines to make the mouth

Earrings made from pleated card

Scrap collage

It's fun to mix different materials and objects in a collage. Here's how to make a picture from scrap materials you may find around your home.

You will need:
- Thick cardboard for the backing sheet
- Objects and materials for the collage (see below)
- Gold or silver spray

Paper clips

Tin foil

Fabric background

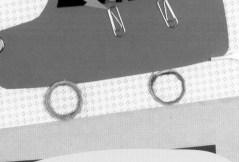

Street scene made from scrap materials

Collage materials

Look out for these scrap materials to use in your collage:

- Buttons and shells
- String, wool and elastic bands
- Scraps of cardboard
- Fabric, ribbon and thread
- Washers, nuts, bolts, nails or screws
- Sponges and corks
- Twigs, feathers and leaves
- Tin foil and bottle tops
- Bubble wrap, cellophane and foam polystyrene

Junk car

Screws

This car was made from scrap materials glued to corrugated cardboard. It was then spray-painted silver.

Small coins and bottle-top wheels

1 Draw the outline of a car on the backing sheet with a pencil.

2 Using safety scissors, cut shapes out of paper, card or thin plastic to fit parts of the car, or arrange items such as buttons, nails or washers in rows.

3 Keep arranging and re-arranging the shapes until you are happy with the way they look.

4 Glue down your collage, one small area at a time.

Click for Art!

To see a collage using scrap plastic and other materials, go to **www.tate.org.uk** click on 'Collection', then search on 'Tony Cragg' and 'Britain Seen from the North'.

Food collage

Use dried foods, glued to a strong cardboard backing sheet, to make an imaginative food collage!

You will need:

- Dried foods (see box)
- Black sugar paper
- Strong cardboard for the backing sheet
- White or yellow pencil
- Tweezers

1 Glue the black sugar paper onto a strong cardboard backing sheet.

Food collage ideas

Food collages work best if you choose a simple pattern or picture. For example:

★ a flower
★ a tiger
★ a lizard
★ a snake with a zigzag pattern on its back

2 Plan your picture on a piece of white paper first. When you are happy with it, draw it onto the sugar paper with a white or yellow pencil.

3 Choose dried foods for the different parts of your picture. Sprinkle a few lentils, beans or seeds in each area to remind you what goes where.

Top tip

Ask an adult to spray the finished collage with glue or lacquer to keep the dried food in place.

Food collage with border made from pasta wheels

5 Leave the collage flat until the glue has dried completely.

4 Spread glue thickly over a small part of the picture. Sprinkle small seeds over the glue. You may find it easier to position larger items with tweezers.

Dried foods

- Red and green lentils
- Dried beans and peas
- Pasta shapes and spaghetti
- Black, white and brown rice
- Sunflower and poppy seeds
- Pine nuts

17

Fabric collage

Collages made out of different fabrics are great to look at – and to touch!

Clouds made from scraps of net curtain

Sheep's soft coats made from wool

You will need:

- Scraps of fabric
- Thick needle and thread (optional)
- Thick cloth or cardboard for the backing sheet

Collecting fabrics

Look out for fabrics with different textures, such as scratchy hessian, smooth silks and soft furs. See what you can find at jumble sales, or cut up old clothes – but always check with an adult first!

1 Plan your picture and draw it lightly onto the backing sheet.

2 Using safety scissors, cut the fabric into shapes.

Click for Art!

To see fabrics used in a collage, go to
www.makleindesign.com/AdvancedFabricCollageideas.htm

Flowers made from scrunched-up scraps of brightly coloured fabric

Working with fabrics

You can use fabrics in a similar way to paper:

⚠️

- **Pleating:** Glue the fabric down as you pleat it, or tack it with big rough stitches using a needle and thread.
- **Scrunching:** Crumple the fabric and glue it down.
- **Twisting:** Twist the fabric, then glue it in place.
- **Plaiting:** Plait strands of different fabrics into one thick strand.
- **Cutting:** Cut fabric into shapes to stick onto another material, or cut holes so you can see through to the fabric below.

3 Arrange the shapes on the backing sheet until you are happy with the way they look. See the pink box for ways of giving your collage an interesting 3-D effect.

4 Glue down the shapes, one small area at a time.

Straw weaving

Woven cloth is good to use in a collage especially if you weave it yourself! To get started, here's how to make a woven wall-hanging using wool and plastic straws.

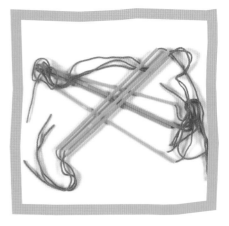

You will need:
- Plastic straws
- Thick cardboard
- Wool, string or embroidery thread for weaving

I Take some plastic straws and thread a length of wool through each one. The wool should be 20cm longer than the straws.

Push this straw down to tighten the threads

Add a second colour to make stripes

Top tip
Try wrapping the wool around a strip of card – this makes it easier to push the threads in and out of the straws.

4 Weave a straw at the top and bottom to hold your threads in place. Your decoration is now ready to hang on the wall.

2 Knot the ends of the wool loosely together at the top and bottom. Then tape the knots to a sheet of cardboard. Make sure the straws lie flat.

3 Weave wool in and out of the straws from left to right, then right to left. If you like, make some stripes using different-coloured wools.

Making a simple loom

ere's how to
t up a simple
rdboard **loom** for
e weaving project
n page 22.

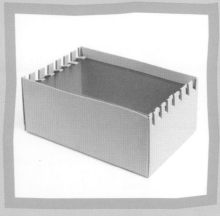

You will need:
- A shoebox
- Wool or string for weaving

1 Ask an adult to help you make a series of notches 1.5cm deep and 1.5cm apart in the sides of a shoebox.

2 Tape the end of a long piece of wool or string to one side of the box. Wrap the wool or string round and round the box, using the notches to hold it in place. These are your **warp** threads.

3 Cut the end of the wool and tape it to the side of the box.

Now turn to page 22 to get weaving!

Woven fabric collage

Use the simple cardboard loom on page 21 to weave fun fabrics for your pictures and collages.

You will need:
- Cardboard loom strung with warp threads (see page 21)
- A strip of strong card
- Wool or cotton thread in different colours

1 Wind a long piece of wool around a strip of strong card that you can easily hold in your fingers. Tie the loose end of the wool around the first warp thread on your loom.

2 Using the card, weave the wool under and over each of the warp threads to form the **weft**.

3 At the end of each row, pull the weft threads down towards you using your fingers.

Top tip
Wind a long thread firmly around each warp thread at the top and bottom of the loom. This gives a neat, strong edge to your woven cloth.

Click for Art!

To see examples of beautiful woven carpets, go to **http://weavingartmuseum.org/main.html**

4 Keep weaving until you have covered all the long warp threads. Knot the loose end of the weft thread.

5 Cut the warp threads on the bottom of the box. Knot the threads together. Cut off the extra string or leave it as a fringe.

Fabric collage

Use woven cloth as the background for a fabric collage.

1 Weave strips of fabric and wool between your warp threads to make bands of different colours and textures.

2 Cut out shapes from felt, such as a moon, star and a boat.

3 Glue the fabric shapes onto your **tapestry** with fabric glue, or ask an adult to help you sew them on.

Glossary

acrylic   easy-to-mix paint that can be cleaned with soap and water

backing sheet   piece of cardboard or paper on which things are stuck down

corrugated   type of cardboard shaped into folds with a pattern of ridges and grooves

loom   device used to weave fibres (such as wool or cotton) together to make cloth or fabric

PVA glue   strong white glue that does not wash away

sugar paper   thick, textured paper often used in scrapbooks

tapestry   cloth that has been woven on a frame

texture   the surface or 'feel' of something – for example, rough, soft, smooth or furry

theme   the subject of something, such as an idea for a story

warp   threads strung across a loom

weave   to make cloth by passing threads or strands under and over each other

weft   threads crossing over and under the warp threads on a loom

Index